The Barking Lot
Underwater Coloring Book 2

The Barking Lot
Underwater Coloring Book 2

KF Wheatie & KM Wheatie

Strawberryhead & Gingerbread Press

www.strawberryheadandgingerbread.com

The Barking Lot Underwater Coloring Book 2

Published by Strawberryhead and Gingerbread Press
https://www.strawberryheadandgingerbread.com

Copyright © 2024 by KF Wheatie & KM Wheatie

All rights reserved. Neither this book, nor any parts within it may be sold or reproduced in any form or by any electronic or mechanical means, including information storage and retrieval systems, without permission in writing from the author. The only exception is by a reviewer, who may quote short excerpts in a review.

ISBN: 979-8-9906129-2-1 (paperback)

Blue whales are the biggest animals in the world. Blue whales eat tiny shrimp like animals called krill. They make loud sounds.

Squid

Squids can squirt ink to escape from predators & change colors to blend in with their surroundings. They are super fast swimmers.

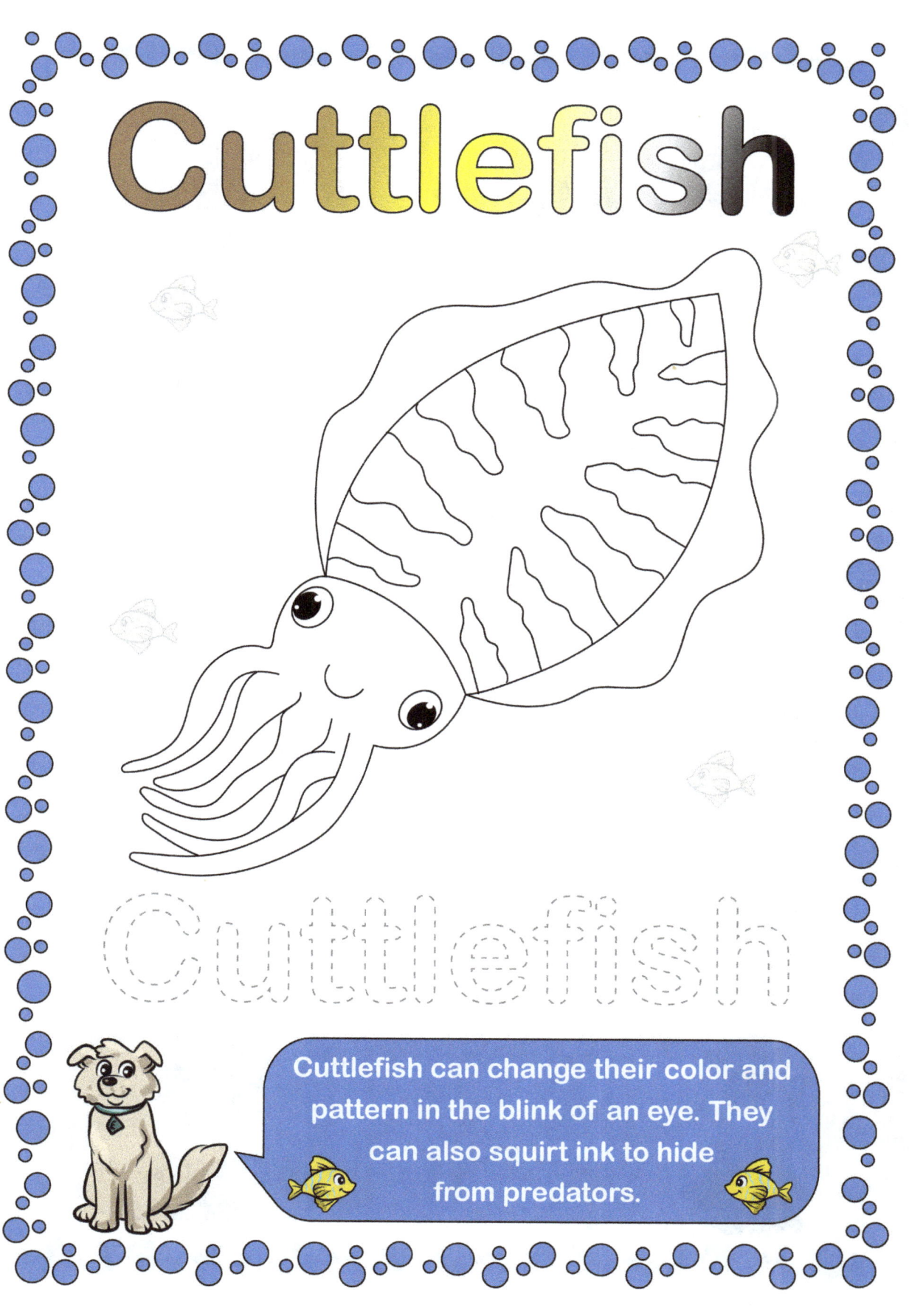

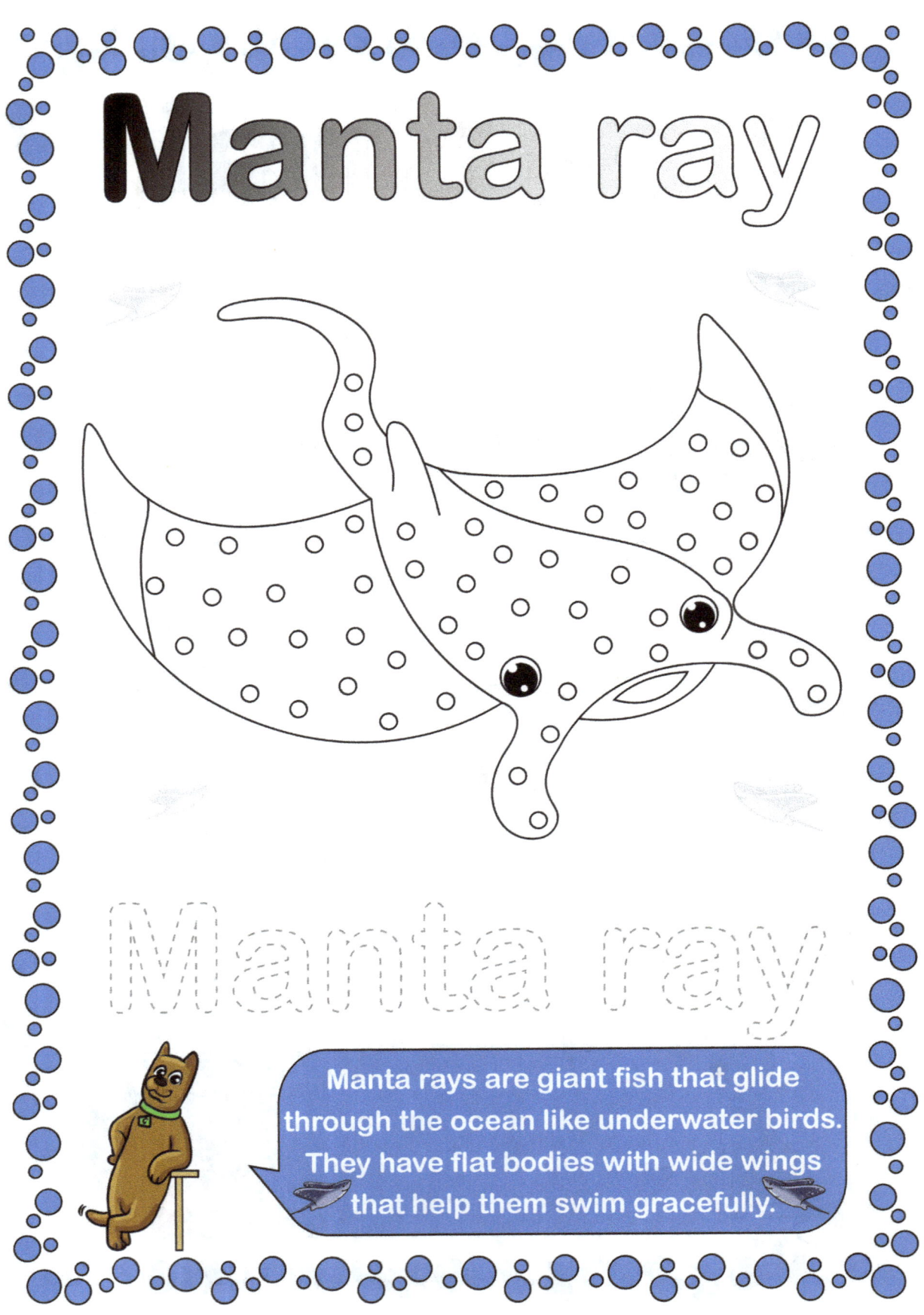

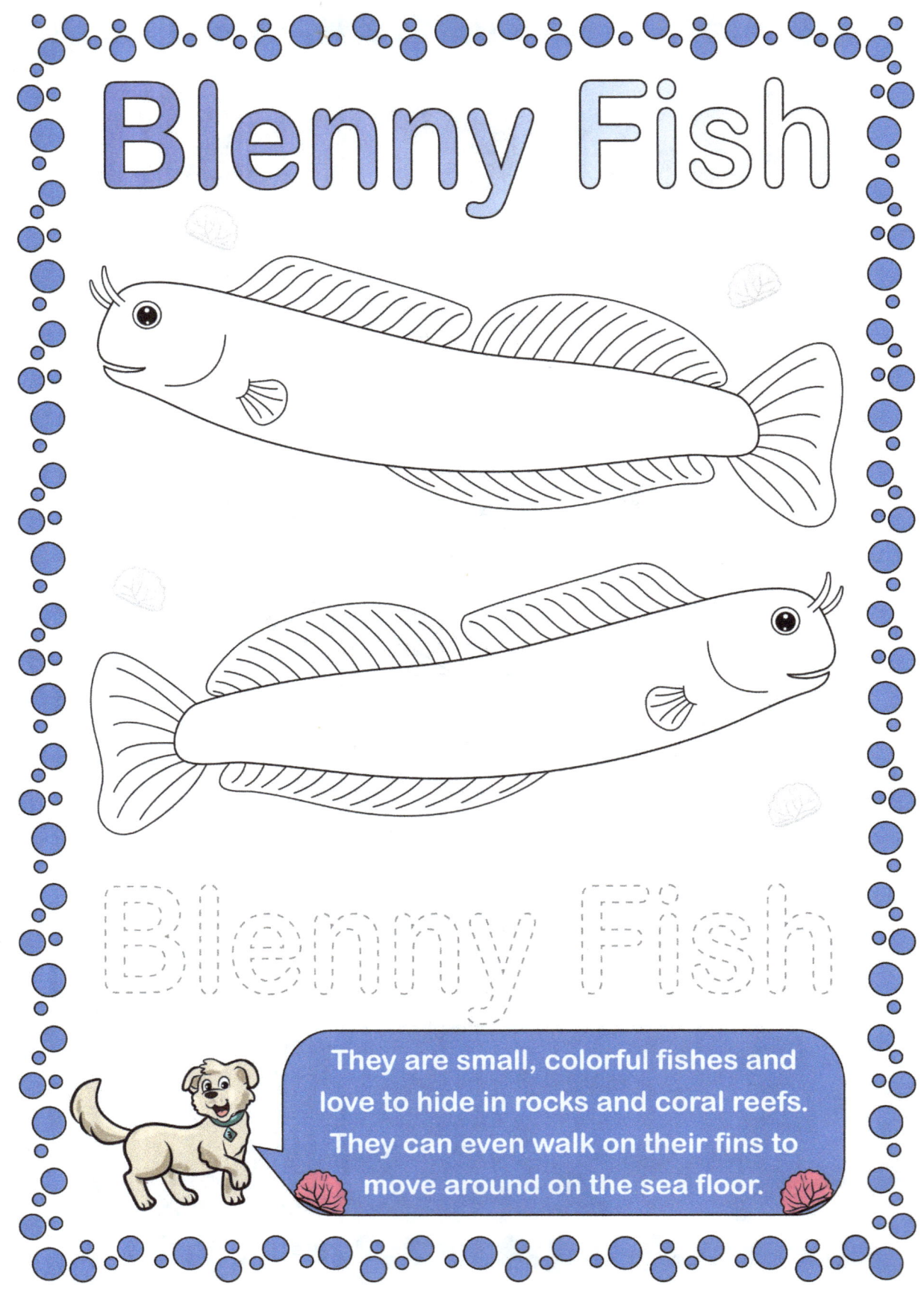

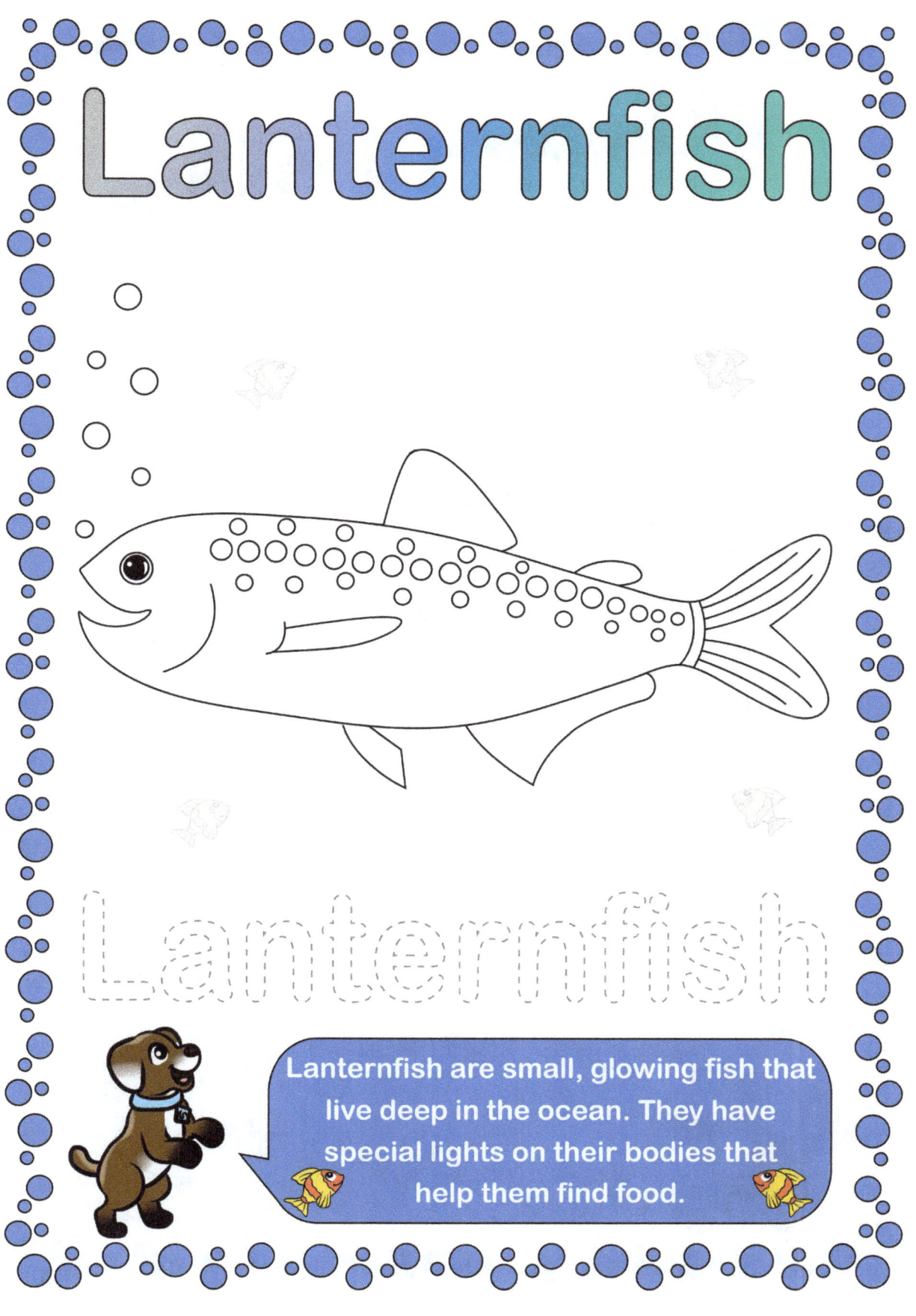

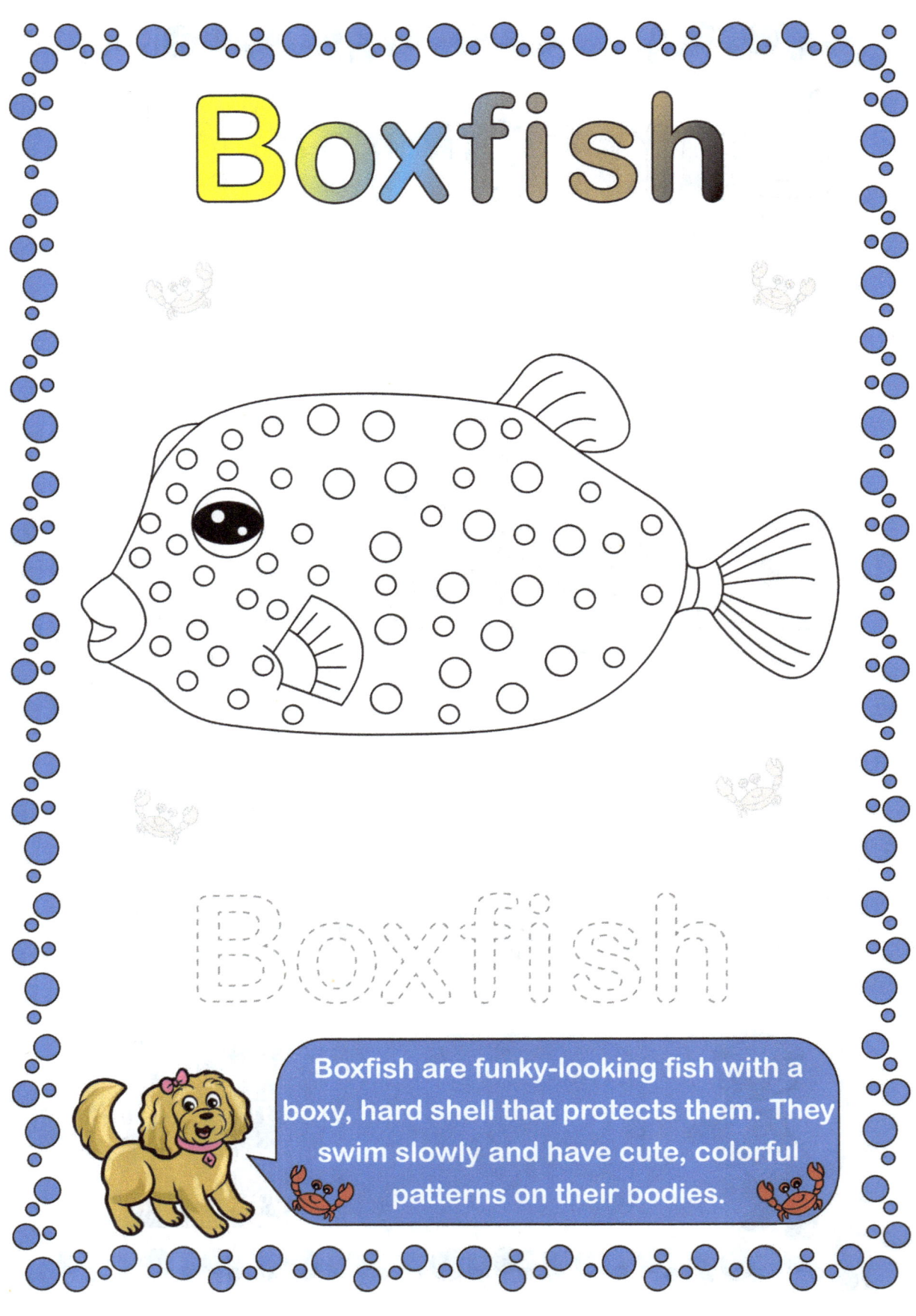

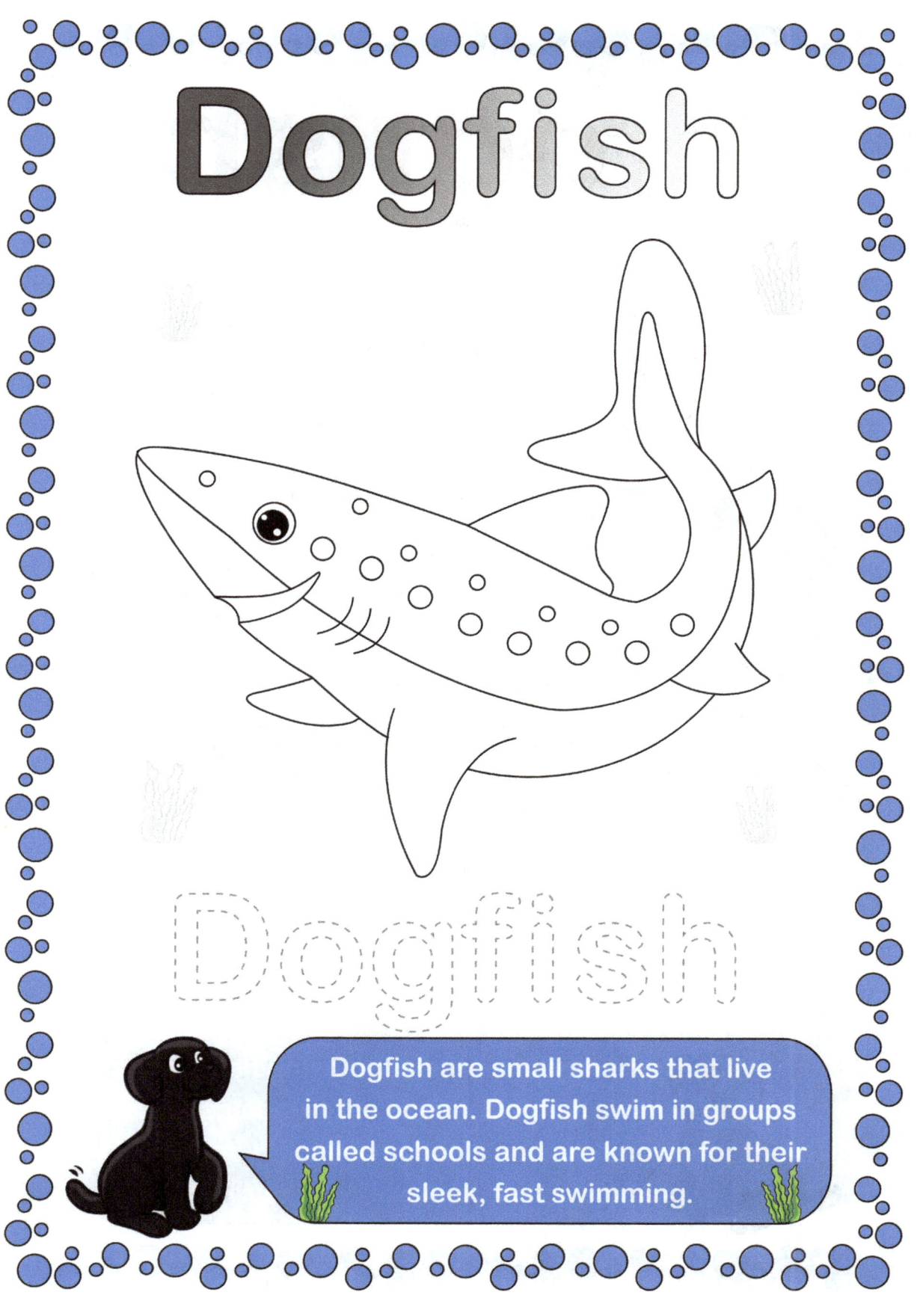

Halibut

Halibut are big, flat fish that live on the ocean floor. They have both eyes on one side of their head and can change color to blend in with the sand.

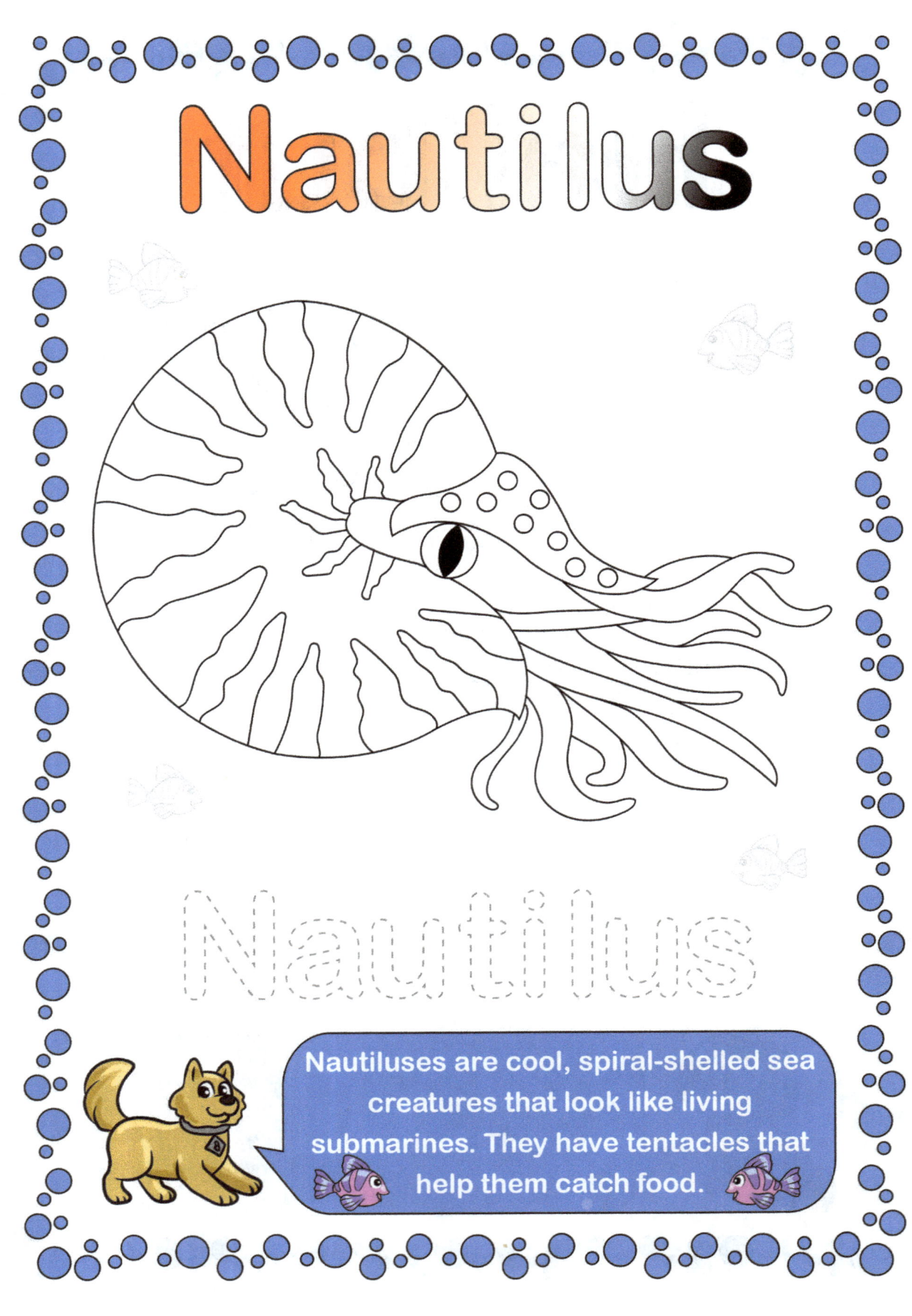

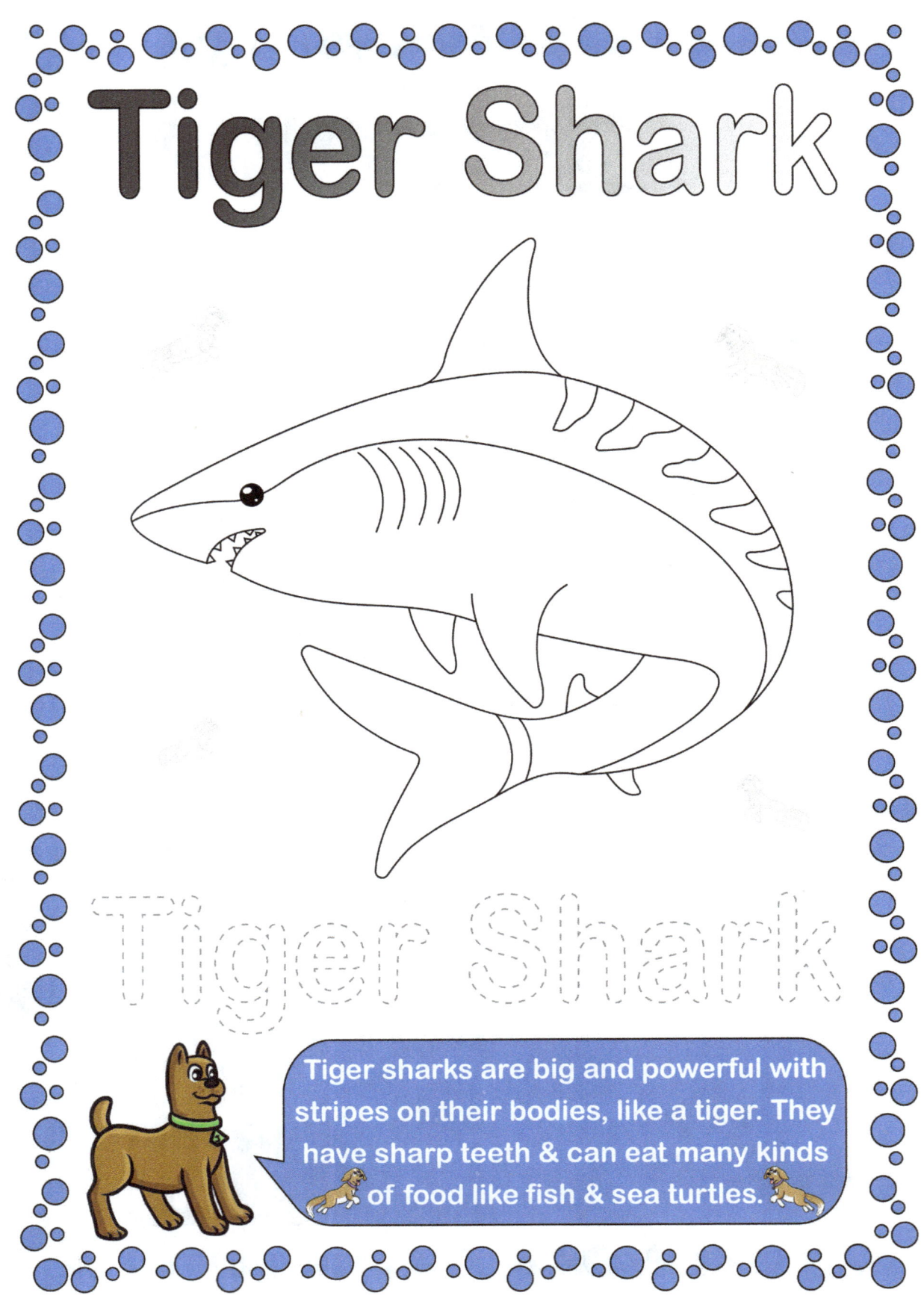

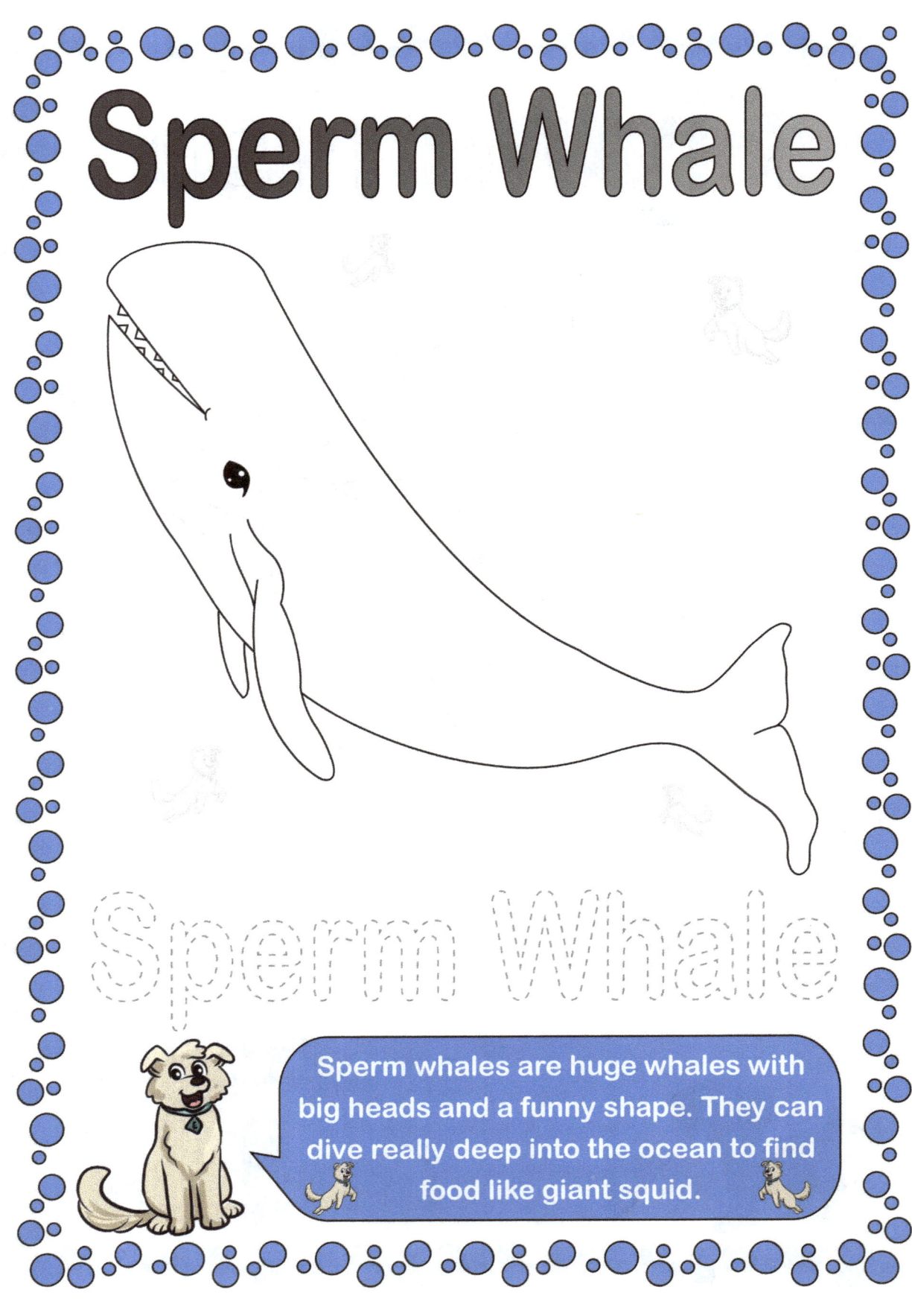

Pipefish

Pipefish are long, skinny fish that look like little underwater pencils. They have a tube-like body and tiny fins that help them swim.

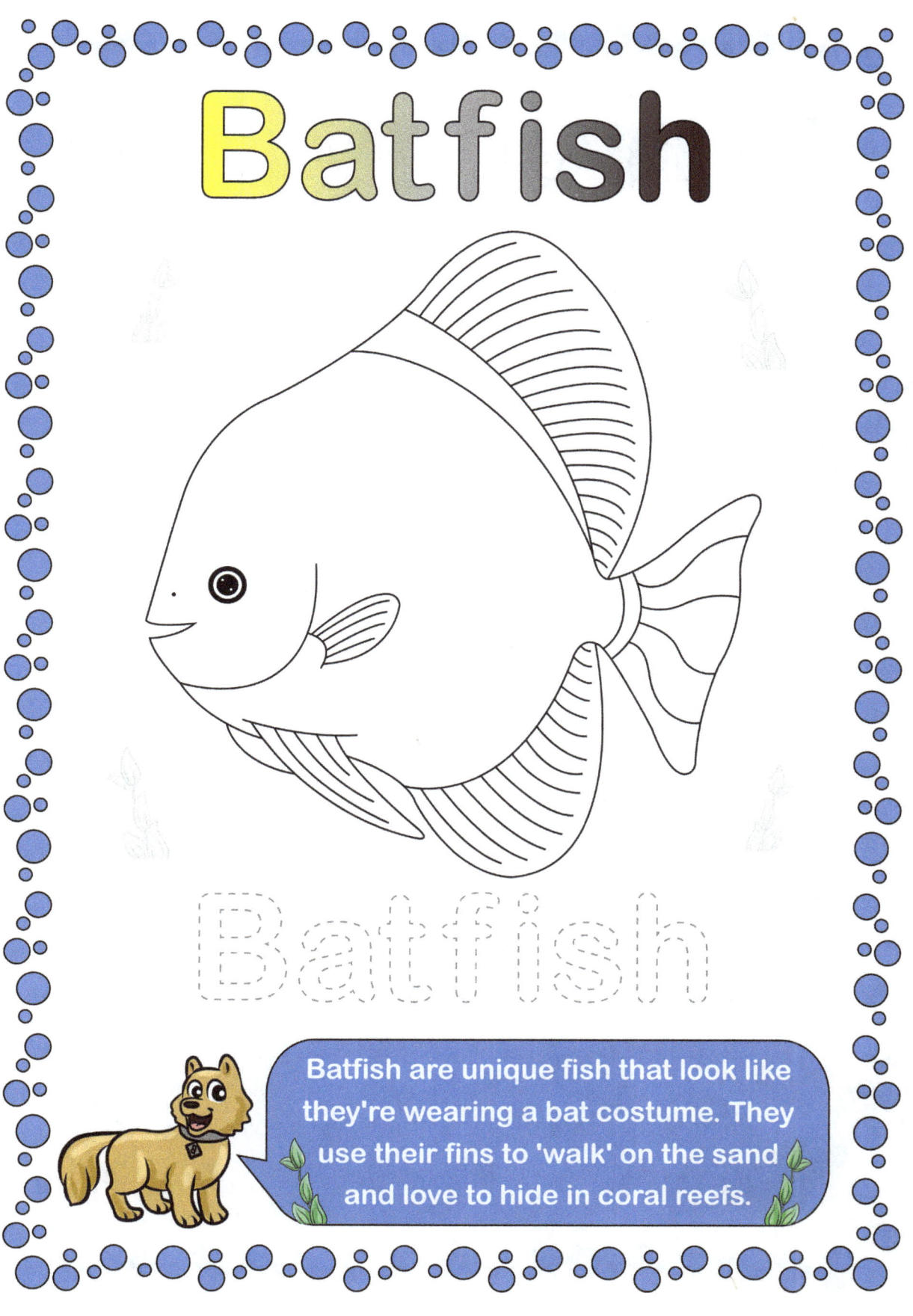

www.ingramcontent.com/pod-product-compliance
Lightning Source LLC
Chambersburg PA
CBHW080536030426
42337CB00023B/4753